Night LIGHTS for Dads

New Leaf Press

First Printing: March 2004

Cover and interior design by Brent Spurlock
Edited by Jim Fletcher and Roger Howerton

ISBN: 0-89221-569-0
Library of Congress Catalog Card Number: 2003116014

Please visit our web site for more great titles:
www.newleafpress.net

New Leaf Press

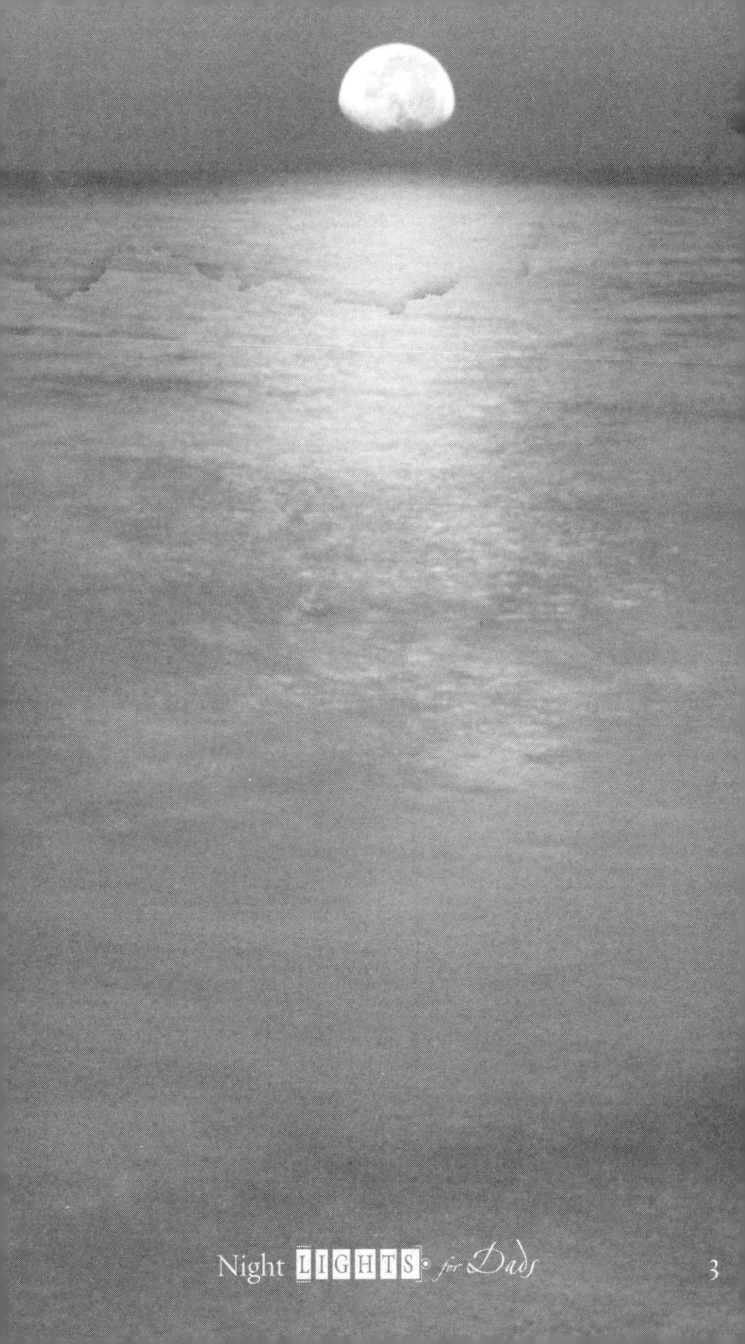

A special gift for you

To

_____

From

_____

It's NOT All That Bad

Most nice respectable American churches don't talk about sin, judgment, or hell. Why? Because they are post-modern. Most Americans read the Bible selectively, omitting those parts they don't like. The first thing many American churchgoers throw out is the concept of hell, because (in their view) a nice, well-behaved God wouldn't let anybody go to hell.

After you lose hell, you lose a sense of sin. Nobody is guilty of anything. Everybody is just a victim. Finally, the call to repent has no meaning. Dr. Calvin Miller of the Beeson Divinity School claims that instead of repenting we play a nice little game entitled, "It's not all that bad." It sounds like this.

"Yes, I did have a brief affair, but my wife was not meeting my needs. I didn't divorce her, so don't call it adultery; it's not all that bad."

"Yes, my daughter and her fiancé share the same bedroom when they visit us, but most engaged couples do. After all, this is the 21st century; it's not all that bad."

"Sure, I sometimes drink too much, but never in front of the kids. I don't do any harm and it never causes me to miss a day of work. It's not all that bad."

Sadly, many American churchgoers live in a state of denial.

TODAY ...

TOMORROW ...

Write down your thoughts and goals.

Woe unto them that call evil good, and good evil; that put darkness for light, and light for darkness; that put bitter for sweet, and sweet for bitter!

– Isaiah 5:20

At the final bar of judgement, the

gravest charge that will be made

against us Christians will be that

we were so unconcerned.

– D. Martyn Lloyd-Jones

An Educated HEART

W̲ e come by business naturally in our
family. Each of the seven children in our
family worked in our father's store, "Our Own
Hardware-Furniture Store," in Mott, North
Dakota, a small town on the prairie. We started
working by doing odd jobs like dusting, arranging
shelves and wrapping, and later graduated to
serving customers. As we worked and watched,
we learned that work was about more than
survival and making a sale. One lesson stands out
in my mind.

It was shortly before Christmas. I was in
the eighth grade and was working evenings,
straightening the toy section. A little boy, five or
six years old, came in. He was wearing a brown
tattered coat with dirty worn cuffs. His hair was
straggly, except for a cowlick that stood straight
up from the crown of his head. His shoes were
scuffed and his one shoelace was torn.

The little boy looked poor to me — too

poor to afford to buy anything. He looked around the toy section, picked up this item and that, and carefully put them back in their place.

Dad came down the stairs and walked over to the boy. His steel blue eyes smiled and the dimple in his cheek stood out as he asked the boy what he could do for him.

The boy said he was looking for a Christmas present to buy his brother. I was impressed that Dad treated him with the same respect as any adult. Dad told him to take his time and look around.

He did.

After about 20 minutes, the little boy carefully picked up a toy plane, walked up to my dad and said, "How much for this, Mister?"

"How much you got?" Dad asked.

The little boy held out his hand and opened

it. His hand was creased with wet lines of dirt from clutching his money. In his hand lay two dimes, a nickel, and two pennies — 27 cents. The price on the toy plane he'd picked out was $3.98.

"That 'll just about do it," Dad said as he closed the sale. Dad's reply still rings in my ears.

I thought about what I'd seen as I wrapped the present. When the little boy walked out of the store, I didn't notice the dirty, worn coat, the straggly hair, or the single torn shoelace. What I saw was a radiant child with a treasure. I also saw my father's educated heart.

TODAY ...

TOMORROW ...

Write down your thoughts and goals.

> *Oh that men would praise the LORD for his goodness, and for his wonderful works to the children of men!*
>
> – Psalm 107:8

Christianity demands a level of

caring that transcends human

inclinations.

– Erwin W. Lutzer

What Does A FATHER Do?

I received a letter from a single mother who had raised a son who was about to become a dad. Since he had no recollection of his own father, her question to me was "What do I tell him a father does?"

When my dad died in my ninth year, I, too, was raised by my mother, giving rise to the same question, "What do fathers do?" As far as I could observe, they brought around the car when it rained so everyone else could stay dry.

They always took the family pictures, which is why they were never in them. They carved turkeys on Thanksgiving, kept the car gassed up, weren't afraid to go into the basement, mowed the lawn, and tightened the clothesline to keep it from sagging.

It wasn't until my husband and I had children that I was able to observe firsthand what a father contributed to a child's life. What did he do to deserve his children's respect? He rarely fed them, did anything about their sagging diapers, wiped their noses or fannies, played ball, or bonded with them under the hoods of their cars.

What did he do?

He threw them higher than his head until they were weak from laughter. He cast the deciding vote on the puppy debate. He listened more than he talked. He let them make mistakes. He allowed them to fall from their first two-wheeler without having a heart attack. He read a newspaper while they were trying to parallel park a car for the first time in preparation for their driving test.

If I had to tell someone's son what a father really does that is important, it would be that he shows up for the job in good times and bad times. He's a man who is constantly being observed by his children. They learn from him how to handle adversity, anger, disappointment, and success.

He won't laugh at their dreams no matter how impossible they might seem. He will go out at 1 a.m. when one of his children runs out of gas. He will make unpopular decisions and stand by them. When he is wrong and makes a mistake, he will admit it. He sets the tone for how family members treat one another, members of the opposite sex and people who are different than they are. By example, he can instill a desire to give something back to the community when its needs are greater than theirs.

But mostly, a good father involves himself in his kids' lives. The more responsibility he has for a child, the harder it is to walk out of his life.

A father has the potential to be a powerful force in the life of a child.

Grab it! Maybe you'll get a greeting card for your efforts. Maybe not. But it's steady work.[1]

**T**ODAY ... _____

_____

_____

_____

_____

_____

_____

_____

_____

_____

_____

_____

_____ **T**OMORROW ...

_____

_____

_____

_____

Write down your thoughts and goals.

> As ye know how we exhorted and
> comforted and charged every one of you,
> as a father doth his children.
> –I Thessalonians 2:11

The father's most important

responsibility is to communicate

the real meaning of Christianity to

his children.

– James Dobson

Death of a STATESMAN

On the morning of July 2, 1881, President James Garfield was shot by Charles Guiteau at the railroad station in Washington. Two bullets were fired, and the first bullet entered Garfield's body from the back and lodged deeply inside, while the second grazed his left arm. The fallen president never lost consciousness and, after some time, asked to be moved to the White House. The ten doctors that had gathered by now at the depot carefully placed him on a mattress and removed him to the executive mansion.

At the White House, 16 doctors, including the surgeon generals of the army and navy, began trying to find the bullet that was lodged in the president's body. X-rays had not yet been invented, so the doctors tried to locate the bullet with the only method known at the time

— probing. One doctor after another probed the wound with his finger, trying to feel the bullet. The doctors never found it, but in Boston, Alexander Graham Bell, who had had great success with his invention of the telephone, heard of the hidden bullet, and asked if he could try to find the bullet with his new invention — the metal detector.

In the early evening of July 26, Bell arrived at the White House with his metal detector. The metal detector had been tested and proven to work accurately with every test to which it had been subjected. Oddly enough, however, when it was used this time, it seemed to be detecting metal everywhere in the president's body. The scientist was puzzled. He made some slight adjustments and tried again. And again. And again.

Nothing. He left the White House that night thoroughly perplexed.

After more testing, Bell returned to the White House on the last day of July. Once again he performed the procedure on Garfield, and the machine acted precisely as it had before. Bell was utterly dumbfounded. Why had the metal detector worked perfectly in every test at the lab, but failed in every use on the president? Bell gave up and silently went back to Boston.

The bullet was never found and President James Garfield died on September 19, 1881.

And what about the failed metal detector? Why hadn't it worked? Well, the late nineteenth century was certainly an age of invention – not only telephones and metal detectors, but there was another new invention as well. Actually, the metal detector had performed perfectly when used on the president. There was nothing wrong with it. That other new invention was the reason that the metal detector had seemed to fail. That other invention was so new that it had not been officially marketed yet, but one had been sent to the chief executive for his early approval and endorsement. Had the president been lying on the floor, reclining in a chair, or lying on a feather bed, the metal detector would have located the bullet, but President Garfield was stretched out on a comfortable new invention, a coil spring mattress – full of metal.

TODAY ...

TOMORROW ...

Write down your thoughts and goals.

"Take us the foxes, the little foxes,
that spoil the vines...."
– Song of Solomon 2:15

It has long been an axiom of mine

that the little things are infinitely

the most important.

– Arthur Conan Doyle

MOTIVATION

E very morning when the sun comes up, a gazelle wakes. He knows that he must outrun the fastest lion or he will be eaten. When the sun comes up, the lion wakes. He knows that he must outrun the slowest gazelle, or he will starve. In the end it doesn't matter whether you are a lion or gazelle; when the sun comes up, you better be running.[2]

Know ye not that they which run in a race run all, but one receiveth the prize? So run, that ye may obtain.
— 1 Corinthians 9:24

TODAY ...

TOMORROW ...

Write down your thoughts and goals.

NOTE Time to Spare

A minister parked his car in a no-parking zone in a large city because he was short of time and couldn't find a space with a meter. He placed a note under the windshield wiper that read: "I have circled the block ten times. If I don't park here, I'll miss my appointment. FORGIVE US OUR TRESPASSES."

When he returned, he found a citation from a police officer along with the following note: "I've circled this block for ten years. If I don't give you a ticket, I'll lose my job. LEAD US NOT INTO TEMPTATION."

Obey them that have the rule over you, and submit yourselves: for they watch for your souls, as they that must give account, that they may do it with joy, and not with grief: for that is unprofitable for you.

– Hebrews 13:17

TODAY ...

_____

_____

_____

_____

_____

_____

_____

_____

_____

_____

_____

TOMORROW ...

_____

_____

_____

_____

_____

Write down your thoughts and goals

LINCOLN'S PROCLAMATION
ON PRAYER

We have been the recipients of the choicest bounties of heaven. We have been preserved, the many years, in peace and prosperity. We have grown in numbers, wealth and power, as no other nation has ever grown. But we have forgotten God.

We have forgotten the gracious hand which preserved us in peace and multiplied and enriched and strengthened us; and we have vainly imagined, in the deceitfulness of our hearts that all these blessings were produced by some superior wisdom and virtue of our own.

Intoxicated with unbroken success, we have become too self-sufficient to feel the necessity of redeeming and preserving grace, too proud to pray to God that made us.

It behooves us, then to humble ourselves before the offended Power, to confess our national sins, and to pray for clemency and forgiveness.[3]

Today ...

Tomorrow ...

Write down your thoughts and goals.

Enter into his gates with thanksgiving, and into his courts with praise: be thankful unto him, and bless his name.

– Psalm 100:4

True prayer is born out of

brokenness.

– Frances J. Roberts

WHAT WE HAVE TAUGHT THE COMING GENERATION

I n Seattle, two 15-year-old boys and their 14-year-old girlfriends decided to skip school and spend the day together. When they missed the bus that would have taken them to the mall, they carjacked an automobile parked in the school zone. It was of no consequence to them that a two-year-old child and an eight-month-old baby were strapped into car seats in the back seat. Ignoring the screams of the mother who held onto the back door handle of the car until the speeding car threw her off, they abandoned the car and the children in a parking lot where they were not found for five hours. . . . Due to no effort of the car-jackers, the children were saved.

When they were found, the shocked parents of the young criminals protested that they were really "good kids."

And last year, in Miami, a 15 year old and his 17-year-old brother, decided to celebrate their parents' absence over a weekend by cruising the streets in the family Mercedes shooting six-inch long spear darts into the backs of elderly black pedestrians.

When they were found, the boys' parents wept before TV cameras, apologizing for the boys' behavior and insisting, "They're really good kids." The eldest of the boys also expressed a concern that this incident might hurt his chances of getting into a good college in the fall.

In Los Angeles, four buddies between the ages of 14 and 17 started out an evening of vandalism by beating mailboxes with a baseball bat. As the evening progressed, they become bolder and started beating out the windows of parked cars and then started hitting people. They loaded up their paintball guns and drove past crowds, indiscriminately shooting at women, the elderly and children, squealing with delight with every hit.

How do we know so much about their evening's escapades? They videotaped their outing themselves so that they could enjoy their night out over and over again.

These were not boys who were usually in trouble. They were described as being "good kids."

James Baldwin, an American author of this century, once said that "Children have never been very good at listening to their elders, but they have never failed to imitate them." I have not cited these few news-clippings as a way of bashing teenagers. I mention these morally empty events as a sign of what we have taught the coming generation. We have somehow lost a sense that we have a higher accountability.[4]

T ODAY...

T OMORROW...

Write down your thoughts and goals.

...that the generation to come might know them, even the children which should be born; who should arise and declare them to their children: That they might set their hope in God, and not forget the works of God, but keep his commandments.

– Psalm 78:6-7

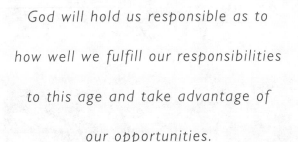

God will hold us responsible as to

how well we fulfill our responsibilities

to this age and take advantage of

our opportunities.

– Billy Graham

Eisenhower on PRAYER

Personal prayer, it seems to me, is one of the simplest necessities of life, as basic to the individual as sunshine, food and water — and at times, of course, more so. By prayer I mean an effort to get in touch with the Infinite. We know that our prayers are imperfect. Of course they are. We are imperfect human beings. A thousand experiences have convinced me beyond room of doubt that prayer multiplies the strength of the individual and brings within the scope of his capabilities almost any conceivable objective."[5]

Yet the LORD will command his lovingkindness in the daytime, and in the night his song shall be with me, and my prayer unto the God of my life.
– Psalm 42:8

TODAY ...

TOMORROW ...

Write down your thoughts and goals.

Jack took a long look at his speedometer before slowing down; 73 in a 55 zone. Fourth time in as many months. How could a guy get caught so often? When his car had slowed to 10 miles an hour, Jack pulled over, but only partially. Let the cop worry about the potential traffic hazard. Maybe some other car will tweak his backside with a mirror. The cop was stepping out of his car, the big pad in hand.

Bob? Bob from church? Jack sunk farther into his trench coat. This was worse than the coming ticket. A Christian cop catching a guy from his own church. A guy who happened to be a little eager to get home after a long day at the office. A guy he was about to play golf with tomorrow. Jumping out of the car, he approached a man he saw every Sunday, a man he'd never seen in uniform. "Hi, Bob. Fancy meeting you like this."

"Hello, Jack." No smile.

"Guess you caught me red-handed in a

rush to see my wife and kids."

"Yeah, I guess." Bob seemed uncertain. Good.

"I've seen some long days at the office lately. I'm afraid I bent the rules a bit — just this once." Jack toed at a pebble on the pavement. "Diane said something about roast beef and potatoes tonight. Know what I mean?"

"I know what you mean. I also know that you have a reputation in our precinct." Ouch. This was not going in the right direction. Time to change tactics.

"What'd you clock me at?"

"Seventy. Would you sit back in your car please?"

"Now wait a minute here, Bob. I checked as soon as I saw you. I was barely nudging 65." The lie seemed to come easier with every ticket.

"Please, Jack, in the car."

Flustered, Jack hunched himself through the still-open door. Slamming shut, he stared at the dashboard. He was in no rush to open the window. The minutes ticked by. Bob scribbled away on the pad. Why hadn't he asked for a driver's license? Whatever the reason, it would be a month of Sundays before Jack ever sat near this cop again.

A tap on the door jerked his head to the left. There was Bob, a folded paper in hand. Jack rolled down the window a mere two inches, just enough room for Bob to pass him the slip. "Thanks." Jack could not quite keep the sneer out of his voice. Bob returned to his police car without a word. Jack watched his retreat in the mirror. Jack unfolded the sheet of paper. How much was this one going to cost? Wait a minute. What was this? Some kind of joke? Certainly not a ticket.

Jack began to read:

Dear Jack,

Once upon a time I had a daughter. She was six when killed by a car. You guessed it — a speeding driver. A fine and three months in jail, and the man was free. Free to hug his daughters — all three of them. I only had one, and I'm going to have to wait until Heaven before I can ever hug her again.

A thousand times I've tried to forgive that man. A thousand times I thought I had. Maybe I did, but I need to do it again. Even now. Pray for me. And be careful, Jack, my son is all I have left.

Bob

Jack turned around in time to see Bob's car pull away and head down the road. Jack watched until it disappeared. A full 15 minutes later, he pulled away and drove slowly home, praying for forgiveness and hugging a surprised wife and kids when he arrived.

TODAY ...

TOMORROW ...

Write down your thoughts and goals.

And let us consider one another to provoke
unto love and to good works.
— Hebrews 10:24

The law tells me how crooked

I am. Grace comes along and

straightens me out.

— D.L. Moody

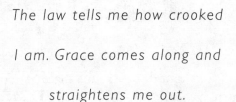

THE UNBAPTIZED ARM

Ivan the Great was the tsar of all of Russia during the fifteenth century. He brought together the warring tribes into one vast empire — the Soviet Union. As a fighting man he was courageous. As a general he was brilliant. He drove out the Tartars and established peace across the nation.

However, Ivan was so busy waging his campaigns that he did not have a family. His friends and advisers were quite concerned. They reminded him that there was no heir to the throne, and should anything happen to him the union would shatter into chaos. "You must take a wife who can bear you a son." The busy soldier and statesman said to them that he did not have the time to search for a bride, but if they would find a suitable one, he would marry her.

The counselors and advisers searched the

capitals of Europe to find an appropriate wife
for the great tsar. And find her, they did. They
reported to Ivan of the beautiful dark eyed
daughter of the king of Greece. She was young,
brilliant, and charming. He agreed to marry her,
sight unseen.

The king of Greece was delighted. It would
align Greece in a favorable way with the
emerging giant of the north. But there had to be
one condition, "He cannot marry my daughter
unless he becomes a member of the Greek
Orthodox Church."

Ivan's response, "I will do it!"

So, a priest was dispatched to Moscow to
instruct Ivan in Orthodox doctrine.

Ivan was a quick student and learned the

catechism in record time. Arrangements were concluded, and the tsar made his way to Athens accompanied by 500 of his crack troops — his personal palace guard.

He was to be baptized into the Orthodox Church by immersion, as was the custom of the Eastern Church. His soldiers, ever loyal, asked to be baptized also. The Patriarch of the Church assigned 500 priests to give the soldiers a one-on-one catechism crash course. The soldiers, all 500 of them, were to be immersed in one mass baptism. Crowds gathered from all over Greece.

What a sight that must have been, 500 priests and 500 soldiers, a thousand people, walking into the blue Mediterranean. The priests were dressed in black robes and tall black hats, the official dress of the Orthodox Church. The soldiers wore their battle uniforms with of all their regalia — ribbons of valor, medals of courage. and their weapons of battle.

Suddenly, there was a problem. The Church prohibited professional soldiers from being members; they would have to give up their commitment to bloodshed. They could not be killers and church members too.

After a hasty round of diplomacy, the problem was solved quite simply. As the words were spoken and the priests began to baptize them, each soldier reached to his side and withdrew his sword. Lifting it high overhead, every soldier was totally immersed — everything baptized except his fighting arm and sword.

TODAY ...

TOMORROW ...

Write down your thoughts and goals.

Jesus said unto him, Thou shalt love the Lord thy God with all thy heart, and with all thy soul, and with all thy mind. This is the first and great commandment.

– Matt. 22:37-38

The greatness of a man's power is

the measure of his surrender.

– William Booth

What GOD Is Like

A small boy was consistently late coming home from school. His parents warned him that he must be home on time that afternoon, but nevertheless he arrived later than ever. His mother met him at the door and said nothing. His father met him in the living room and said nothing.

At dinner that night, the boy looked at his plate. There was a slice of bread and a glass of water. He looked at his father's full plate and then at his father, but his father remained silent. The boy was crushed.

The father waited for the full impact to sink

in, then quietly took the boy's plate and placed it in front of himself. He took his own plate of meat and potatoes, put it in front of the boy, and smiled at his son.

When that boy grew to be a man, he said, "All my life I've known what God is like by what my father did that night."[6]

TODAY ...

TOMORROW ...

Write down your thoughts and goals.

For God so loved the world, that he gave his only begotten Son, that whosoever believeth in him should not perish, but have everlasting life.

— John 3:16

Grace is the central invitation to life and the final word. It's the beckoning nudge and the overwhelming, undeserved mercy that urges us to change and grow, and then gives us the power to pull it off.

— Tim Hansel

Church HYMNS

One Sunday a pastor told his congregation that the church needed some extra money and asked the people to prayerfully consider giving a little extra in the offering plate.

After the offering plates were passed, the pastor glanced down and noticed that someone had placed a $1,000 bill in offering. He was so excited that he immediately shared his joy with his congregation and said he'd like to personally thank the person who placed the money in the plate.

A very quiet, elderly, saintly lady all the way in the back shyly raised her hand. The pastor asked her to come to the front. Slowly she made her way to the pastor. He told her how wonderful it was that she gave so much and in thanksgiving asked her to pick out three hymns.

Her eyes brightened as she looked over the congregation, pointed to the three handsomest men in the building and said, "I'll take him and him and him."

TODAY...

TOMORROW...

Write down your thoughts and goals.

> Give, and it shall be given unto you; good measure, pressed down, and shaken together, and running over, shall men give into your bosom. For with the same measure that ye mete withal it shall be measured to you again.
>
> – Luke 6:38

The only safe rule is to give more than we can spare. Our charities should pinch and hamper us. If we live at the same level of affluence as other people who have our level of income, we are probably giving away too little.

– C.S. Lewis

CLEAR CONSCIENCE

In *Inside Sports* John Feinstein writes:

In 1994 golfer Davis Love III called a one-stroke penalty on himself during the second round of the Western Open. He had moved his marker on a green to get it out of another player's putting line. One or two holes later, he couldn't remember if he had moved his ball back to its original spot. Unsure, Love gave himself an extra stroke.

As it turned out, that one stroke caused him to miss the cut and get knocked out of the tournament. If he had made the cut and then finished dead last, he would have earned $2,000 for the week. When the year was over, Love was $590 short of automatically qualifying for the following year's Masters. Love began 1995 needing to win a tournament to get into the event.

When someone asked how much it would bother him if he missed the Masters for calling a penalty on himself, Love's answer was simple: "How would I feel if I won the Masters and wondered for the rest of my life if I cheated to get in?"

The story has a happy ending. The week before the 1995 Masters, Love qualified by winning a tournament in New Orleans. Then in the Masters, he finished second, earning $237,600.

The only truly satisfying reward is one gained honestly, for a guilty conscience can spoil any gain.[7]

TODAY ...

TOMORROW ...

Write down your thoughts and goals.

> *He that speaketh truth sheweth forth*
> *righteousness: but a false witness deceit.*
> — Proverbs 12:17

If one can be certain that his

principles are right, he need not

worry about the consequences.

— *Robert Elliott Speer*

You TALKING to Me?

W hen Lyndon Johnson was president of the United States, one of his aides was Bill Moyers, now of television fame, but then a political consultant and originally an ordained Baptist minister.

One day at a luncheon at the White House, Johnson asked Moyers to give the prayer before the meal. Moyers began his prayer, but Johnson, who was seated at the other end of the table, couldn't hear. So he shouted, "Speak up, Bill. I can't hear you."

And Moyers replied, "Mr. President, I wasn't talking to you."[8]

Be careful for nothing; but in every thing by prayer and supplication with thanksgiving let your requests be made known unto God.
– Philippians 4:6

TODAY ...

TOMORROW ...

Write down your thoughts and goals.

CHRISTMAS ALL YEAR

An attorney I very much admired once said that the greatest gift he ever received in his life was a note his dad gave him on Christmas. It read, "Son, this year I will give you 365 hours. An hour every day after dinner. We'll talk about whatever you want to talk about. We'll go wherever you want to go, play whatever you want to play. It will be your hour." That dad kept his promise and renewed it every year.[9]

... bring them up in the nurture and admonition of the Lord.
— Ephesians 6:4

TODAY ...

_____
_____
_____
_____
_____
_____
_____
_____
_____

TOMORROW ...

_____
_____
_____
_____

Write down your thoughts and goals.

FINISHED THE BOOK

A young man was to be sentenced to the penitentiary. The judge had known him from childhood, for he was well acquainted with his father, a famous legal scholar and the author of an exhaustive study entitled "The Law of Trusts."

"Do you remember your father?" asked the magistrate.

"I remember him well, your honor," came the reply.

Then trying to probe the offender's conscience, the judge said, "As you are about to be sentenced and as you think of your wonderful dad, what do you remember most clearly about him?"

There was a pause. Then the judge received an answer he had not expected.

"I remember when I went to him for advice. He looked up at me from the book he was writing and said, 'Run along, boy; I'm busy!' When I went to him for companionship, he turned me away, saying 'Run along, son; this book must be finished!' Your honor, you remember him as a great lawyer. I remember him as a lost friend."

The magistrate muttered to himself, "Alas! Finished the book, but lost the boy!" [10]

TODAY ...

TOMORROW ...

Write down your thoughts and goals.

> *Fathers, provoke not your children to anger, lest they be discouraged.*
> – Colossians 3:21

The acid test of a father's

leadership is not in the realm of his

social skills, his public relations, his

managerial abilities at the office, or

how well he handles himself before

the public. It is in the home.

– Charles Swindoll

THE RIGHT DECISION

Families don't grow strong unless parents invest precious time in them. In *New Man*, Gary Oliver writes about a difficult decision made by professional baseball player Tim Burke concerning his family:

From the time Burke can first remember, his dream was to be a professional baseball player. Through years of sacrifice and hard work, he achieved that goal.

While a successful pitcher for the Montreal Expos, he and his wife wanted to start a family but discovered they were unable to have children. After much prayer, they decided to adopt four special-needs international children. This led to one of the most difficult decisions of Tim's life.

He discovered that his life on the road conflicted with his ability to be a quality husband and dad. Over time it became clear that he couldn't do a good job at both. After more prayer and soul-searching, he made what many considered an unbelievable decision: he decided to give up professional baseball.

When he left the stadium for the last time, reporters wanted to know why he was retiring. "Baseball is going to do just fine without me," he said. "It's not going to miss a beat. But I'm the only father my children have. I'm the only husband my wife has. And they need me a lot more than baseball does." [11]

TODAY ...

TOMORROW ...

Write down your thoughts and goals.

> *Let thy fountain be blessed: and rejoice with the wife of thy youth.*
>
> – Proverbs 5:18

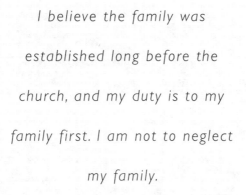

I believe the family was established long before the church, and my duty is to my family first. I am not to neglect my family.

– D.L. Moody

HERO FATHER

One of the most powerful stories in the history of the Olympic games involved a canoeing specialist named Bill Havens. He was a shoo-in, I'm told, to win a gold medal in the 1924 Olympic games in Paris. But a few months before the games were held, he learned that his wife would likely give birth to their first child while he was away. She told him that she could make it on her own, but this was a milestone Bill just didn't want to miss. So he surprised everyone and stayed home. Bill greeted his infant son, Frank, into the world on August 1, 1924. Though he always wondered what might have been, he said he never regretted his decision.

Well, he poured his life into that little lad and shared with him a love for the rapids. Twenty-four years passed, and the Olympic games were held in Helsinki, Finland. This time Frank Havens was chosen to compete in the canoeing event. The day after the competition, Bill received a telegram from his son that read: "Dear Dad, Thanks for waiting around for me to be born in 1924. I'm coming home with the gold medal that you should have won." It was signed, "Your loving son, Frank."

Many would question Bill Haven's decision to miss his big opportunity in Paris, but he never wavered. He wanted his family to know that they always came first, no matter what. And that made him a hero to a little boy named Frank.[12]

TODAY ...

TOMORROW ...

Write down your thoughts and goals.

> *Honour thy father and thy mother: that thy days may be long upon the land which the LORD thy God giveth thee.*
>
> – Exodus 20:12

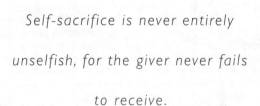

Self-sacrifice is never entirely

unselfish, for the giver never fails

to receive.

– Dolores E. McGuire

BUILD ME A SON

Build me a son, O Lord, who will be strong enough to know when he is weak, and brave enough to face himself when he is afraid; one who will be proud and unbending in honest defeat, and humble and gentle in victory.

Build me a son whose wishbone will not be where his backbone should be; a son who will know Thee and that to know himself is the foundation stone of knowledge. Lead him, I pray, not in the path of ease and comfort, but under the stress and spur of difficulties and challenge. Here let him learn to stand up in the storm; here let him learn compassion for those who fail.

Build me a son whose heart will be clean, whose goal will be high; a son who will master himself before he seeks to master other men; one who will learn to laugh, yet never forget how to weep; one who will reach into the future, yet never forget the past.

And after all these things are his, add, I pray, enough of a sense of humor, so that he may always be serious, yet never take himself too seriously. Give him humility, so that he may always remember the simplicity of greatness, the open mind of true wisdom, the meekness of true strength.

Then I, his father, will dare to whisper, "I have not lived in vain." [13]

TODAY...

TOMORROW...

Write down your thoughts and goals.

> I will declare the decree: the LORD hath
> said unto me, Thou art my Son; this day
> have I begotten thee.
>
> – Psalm 2:7

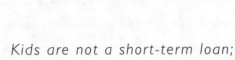

Kids are not a short-term loan;

they are a long-term investment!

– *Anonymous*

LEARNING FROM DAD

Whenever major league baseball player Curt Schilling pitches, he writes his dad's name on the free-ticket list for that game. It's a practice he started in 1988, and he says it will continue as long as he plays the game.

This wouldn't be all that unusual, except that a few months before Curt's major league debut, his dad died of cancer. Putting his father's name on that list is an ongoing tribute to the man who for 22 years provided guidance, instruction, encouragement, and inspiration.

Just as Curt Schilling's dad gave him the incentive to succeed in baseball, so we need to instill in our children the knowledge, desire, and wisdom to succeed in the arena of faith. Nothing is more important than to spend time building into our children the skills to do right in God's eyes.[14]

Oh that men would praise the LORD for his goodness, and for his wonderful works to the children of men!

— Psalm 107:31

TODAY ...

TOMORROW ...

Write down your thoughts and goals.

The bumper sticker states, "My wife says I never pay attention to what she says — or something like that." It's funny, I admit, but the more I think about it, the more I don't want to be that kind of a husband.

Far too many husbands have developed an attitude toward their wives of half-heartedly hearing what they say and not giving them the respect of 100-percent attention.

A husband who does this, or in any way shows disrespect, should consider how his words and deeds also affect his children. After all, he's not just speaking as a husband — he's speaking as a father who needs to teach his children to respect their mother.

In Proverbs 31, the writer mentions that the children of the virtuous woman will "rise up and call her blessed" (v. 28). That kind of honor does not come easily. It comes to a mother who shows good character, but it also comes from children who have been taught by a trusting, loving father how important it is to show respect for Mom.

Husbands and fathers, renew your commitment to love and honor your wife by kind words, thoughtful actions, and respectful communication. Long after the flowers have died and the perfume is gone, that kind of present will continue to be appreciated. And your children will notice too. [15]

TODAY...

TOMORROW...

Write down your thoughts and goals.

> *Her children rise up and call her blessed;*
> *her husband also, and he praises her.*
> — Proverbs 31:28

One of the best ways to

demonstrate God's love is to

listen to people.

— Bruce Larsen

Good TRADE!

My husband, two-month-old daughter and I were flying to Kansas for a family wedding and met up with my father on a connecting flight. He was sitting in business class and felt guilty because we were in coach.

To compensate, Dad made his way to the back of the plane after take-off, bringing with him some first-class goodies and taking my fidgety daughter up front with him for a few minutes. Just then a woman behind me, who had seen the whole thing, leaned forward and asked, "Did you just trade that baby for a couple of packs of pretzels and some cookies?" [16]

I will praise the LORD according to his righteousness: and will sing praise to the name of the LORD most high.

– Psalm 7:17

Today ...

Tomorrow ...

Write down your thoughts and goals.

PORTRAIT OF FATHER

S ome say we never really know another person, that we really have only our perceptions of another while the real person remains a mystery, perhaps even to himself. At no time does this seem truer than after a person's death when perceptions are all that remains. It's a truth that came home to me vividly after my father's death.

My father's office called my mother soon after he died to say they had decided to name one of their conference rooms in his memory. He had been prominent in their firm and they wanted to have a portrait of him to hang in the room. So we sat down, my mother, my brother, my sister and I, and began sorting through boxes and trunks, looking for pictures of him that could be used by the portrait artist.

Curiously, there weren't many. He was fussy about having his picture taken, especially in his later years when he was crippled with arthritis. We finally came up with a handful, ranging from his Air Force picture when he was in his late twenties to a snapshot of him at age 60, sitting, cane in hand, in a lawn chair in the yard.

My brother's artist friend volunteered to do the portrait. We gathered in great anticipation when it was finished and my brother brought it for us to see. It was hideous. The artist started from my father's picture as an old man and tried to shave a few years off him. Dorian Gray's portrait looked better.

So I, the youngest daughter, piped up and suggested that he try again, this time starting with my father's Air Force picture and making it a little older.

A month later the portrait arrived. Everyone stared at it for a long time. My sister, always a very black and white person, announced as soon as she saw it that she didn't like it; it wasn't him. My mother agreed that it looked like his Air Force picture but said she just couldn't remember my father back that far anymore. My brother liked it well enough but he said he really didn't have an eye for these things. He never got along well with Dad so I think he felt that disqualified him.

The firm didn't like the portrait either. The secretaries all remembered him as the wizened old man shuffling to his office. Even his partner of 30 years preferred to remember him that way. So they retained their own artist and commissioned another portrait, the portrait of an old man.

I have the original portrait. It sits on the floor in my office. It's the father I remember from my childhood, the one who suited up and strode out the door every morning to tame dragons when I was small, the one who threw me up in the air, rode me on his shoulders, my first love.

Mind you, I haven't hung it on the wall. It stands on the floor in my office. While I love having him with me while I work, I wouldn't want him getting the impression he's in charge here.

TODAY ...

TOMORROW ...

Write down your thoughts and goals.

> *Does not wisdom cry out, And understanding lift up her voice?*
> — Proverbs 8:1

If God has made your cup

sweet, drink it with grace. If He

has made it bitter, drink it in

communion with Him.

— Oswald Chambers

A BIG JOB

After a big thunderstorm, my daughter helped me shovel mud from our driveway so we could open our gate. Four-year-old Kayla could barely lift the shovel. "This is a big job for such a little girl," she informed me proudly.

She had on her galoshes so when the job was done we decided to look for mud puddles she could stomp around in. After a very satisfying time, we headed for home, hand in hand.

I looked down at her and said, "Have I mentioned today that I love you?"

She giggled, "Yes!" and skipped right out of both of her galoshes. That's when I knew how important daddies can be to little girls.[17]

> *It is good to give thanks to the Lord, And to sing praises to Your name, O Most High: To declare your lovingkindness in the morning, And your faithfulness every night.*
>
> – Psalm 92:1,2

Today ...

_____

_____

_____

_____

_____

_____

_____

_____

_____

_____

_____

Tomorrow ...

_____

_____

_____

_____

_____

Write down your thoughts and goals.

THE WONDER KID

It's tough sometimes to be a dad,
Especially when your kid is bad.
You wonder why she did what she did
— And why she's not a wonder kid.

A wonder kid is always good.
A wonder kid does what she should.
A wonder kid is never bad.
A wonder kid makes daddies glad.

She doesn't shout, she doesn't fight,
She goes to bed on time each night.
She makes her bed, she eats her peas,
She always says, "yes, sir" and "please."

She never whines and never mopes.
She likes to bathe, and uses soap.
She chews her food, she doesn't slurp,
And when she's through she doesn't burp.

She wears her mittens when it freezes.
She's kind to pets and never teases.
She cares for toys and likes to share them.
Her clothes get cleaner as she wears them.

"Did you ever hear of such a kid?"
I asked my kid, who never did.
And then, oh boy, was I surprised
When my little girl apologized:

"I'm sorry for the thing I did.
I wish I were a wonder kid.
I wish that I could make you glad.
I love you so, my wonder Dad."

I hemmed and hawed, I coughed and sputtered,
The butterflies in my stomach fluttered.
I'd focused on her faults, but she
Had only seen the good in me.

It's tough sometimes to be a kid,
Especially when Dad blows his lid.
You wonder how he gets that way,
And why he takes so long to say:

"I love you too, I'm really glad
To know you think I'm a wonder dad,
And I wouldn't change you, not a bit —
You already are a wonder kid."[18]

TODAY ...

_____

_____

_____

_____

_____

_____

_____

_____

TOMORROW ...

_____

_____

_____

_____

_____

Write down your thoughts and goals.

> A wise son makes a glad father, But a foolish
> son is the grief of his mother.
>
> – Proverbs 10:1

A child of God should be a visible

beatitude for joy and happiness,

and a living doxology for gratitude

and adoration.

– Charles Spurgeon

A s I watched his head teeter back and forth, I unconsciously began mimicking the motion. It was just for a few moments, until his eyes slowly shut. The next thing was my son abruptly awakening as his head plopped into his warm mashed potatoes. As he looked up and shook the gravy from his eyebrows, his food-encased face said, "What just happened?"

My only thought at that moment as I spooned him off was to ask, "Was it worth it?" I didn't mean his swan dive into his dinner plate, but the event of the prior night that had left him in this somnolent condition. I was a little tired myself but able to remain erect and keep my mashed potatoes at a safe silverware distance.

It really had all begun a few months earlier. There comes a time in every child's life where they speak those words which cause parents to feel as though they've just sustained a hit to the solar plexus.

The horrifying words are in response to an innocent parental question. Namely, what did they want to do for their birthday party? The earth-shattering reply is short on syllables but ultimately, long on decibels. "Sleepover party" is the response that sends parents clamoring for the safety of a nice party with that friendly mouse character down at Chuck E. Cheese.

If you look up misnomer in the dictionary, the world "sleepover" is provided as a definition. Same with oxymoron. Of course, I was the moron who voluntarily agreed to have 13 ten-year-old boys take over my basement. Sleep has absolutely nothing to do with this phenomenon. Party is the operative term. Party, party, party. The more appropriate name would be a "Yak-yell-and-beep-a-thon."

Now, I must confess that I was a little more

naive than my wife was. She knew fully well what was in store for us if we consented and the matter was opened for debate. I, on the other hand, viewed this simply as a necessary evil for parents to endure and a right of passage for our son. I saw it as something that had been passed down from generation to generation. Something that needed to transpire, lest he experience some twisted and arrested development of maturity.

My wife gave me her quizzical look and calmly responded, "Well, that theory does explain why your maturity level stopped in the early teens. Missed your sleepover birthday party, didn't you honey?"

The fact is I did have one. What I mostly recall is the sugar buzz I had for the next ten days. I was stuck scraping Milk Duds off our ceiling the following morning as well as vacuuming up six tons of rock candy from the floor. All the while I was unable to stop the tune of "Born to be Wild" by Steppenwolf from pounding away in my head. A musical hangover. To this day, I still cringe when

I hear that song and get an uncontrollable desire to do some overly animated air guitar playing and bounce off walls.

My son's party wasn't a whole lot different except for the technological advancements over the last thirty years. The incessant beeping of computer games was only overshadowed by the noise the boys generated playing some strange macabre game involving Raisinettes, licorice, Britanny Spears posters and an inordinate amount of crazy glue. Hey, I figure in a few years I can use the video that I took to my full advantage. A little coercion now and then is all right.

Needless to say I had a little explaining the next day when their parents arrived for pick up. At that time I was still using nail polish remover to try to disengage the candy stuck to their son's body. I was left to clarify for them why their child's sleeping bag appeared permanently attached to my basement ceiling.

I've also got a new song to make me shudder after hearing Lou Bega's "Mambo Number Five" played 417 consecutive times in multiphonic sound. Nothing like numerous portable CD players all simultaneously and ceaselessly playing the same song to get your feet twitching. Or at least your teeth grinding.

And despite my son's somnolent shuffle of the next day, the answer to "Was it worth it?" was a resounding "Yes!" I get to look forward to variations of the same theme with my two younger children. Maybe I can convince them there's as much birthday fun with two friends, a mellow video movie and parental pickup by 10:00 p.m.

But they're probably smarter than to fall for that. Even if it means surviving a face plop into their dinner plate the day after. They'll live with that.[19]

TODAY…

TOMORROW…

Write down your thoughts and goals.

He who keeps instruction is in the way of life,
But he who refuses correction goes astray.
– Proverbs 10:17

Kids can frustrate and irritate

their parents . . . but the rewards

of raising them far outweigh

the cost. Besides, nothing worth

having ever comes cheap.

– James Dobson

TEACHING CHILDREN THE
IMPORTANCE OF WINNING

L ike any devoted father with an ego the size of a banana tree, I prepared for the annual cub scout pine wood derby with the cunning and patience of a lioness in wait. My seven-year-old Tiger cub thought the car we had constructed was "cool." Having been exposed to the rigors of previous derbies with my older son, I knew that many scouts, along with their aerospace engineer fathers, would craft six-inch vehicles that would put Detroit's Big Three to shame. As race time approached, I employed all my creative energy to produce a car that would do my son proud.

The school cafeteria had been converted to a scale model of the Indy 500 Speedway. Checkered flags and Pennzoil posters decorated the walls. A grandstand lined the track, a downhill drag strip that had been electronically wired to capture photo finish winners and display the results on a video projected image on the wall opposite the spectators. This was serious business.

Pre-race festivities included a showcase display of all the cars and, as I had anticipated, many of the cars appeared to be scale replicas of the Formula 1 racers, complete with miniature leather seats and chrome plated stick shifts. Our car fell somewhere between these prima donnas and the unpainted cars that some fathers had the audacity to let their cub scouts make on their own. I was confident that we would make a respectable showing when the wheels hit the track.

My son eagerly watched as our car was placed along side three others at the top of the track. Every car would compete in four separate heats, each time on a different track to eliminate any advantage a particular track might offer. As the wooden starting gate fell, my son cheered as our car began its descent.

It took only a few seconds for the enthusiasm to turn to disappointment. Our car limped weakly through the finish line, dead last of the four cars and not even a serious challenge for third place. The humiliation repeated itself in the subsequent three heats, each time the morale of my little scout dropping ever deeper into an abyss.

After we had retrieved our embarrassment of a car, my son's despair turned to tears. We huddled behind the grandstand, father consoling son in the face of a mutual defeat. Although I was technically responsible for the construction, and therefore the performance, of the car, my son claimed ownership. It was his car. His peers had beaten him in front of parents, siblings and scout leaders. He was humiliated.

My words seemed inadequate at the

moment. I simply held him close and told him I was sorry. His troop leader, seeing us struggle with our defeat, came over and offered a few platitudes about how winning isn't everything and the important thing was to have fun.

Later, as we drove home, I talked further with my son. Winning is important, I said. We should feel bad when we lose. It does matter whether we win or lose. It is fun to compete, but it is more fun to win. Strive to be the best, I said, and don't be satisfied if you're not.

A strong lesson for a seven year old? Yes, but an even stronger lesson for his father. I realized that as adults we often accept mediocrity, we tolerate imperfection. We teach our young to be complacent in defeat, we shelter them from vicissitudes of the competitive urge. By discrediting the importance of winning we breed a generation that is content with sub-optimum performance.

Not everyone can be the winner. Those that are should be congratulated for achieving what we have not. We should then turn our own disappointment into a renewed effort to do better, to keep trying until we can stand in the winner's circle.

My son and I agreed to start early for next year's race. We're determined to bring home a trophy. We'll spend time learning and working together to build the best car we can. That's the whole purpose of the pine wood derby anyway, fathers and sons working together. That, and winning.[20]

TODAY ...

_____

_____

_____

_____

_____

_____

_____

_____

_____

_____

_____

_____

TOMORROW ...

_____

_____

_____

_____

_____

Write down your thoughts and goals.

> *If you have run with the footmen, and they have wearied you, then how can you contend with horses?*
>
> – Jeremiah 12:5

Always imitate the behavior of the

winners when you lose.

— *George Meredith*

JACOB'S RITUAL

Your wailing in the night's silence
Is my patience true test
Removed from my warm bed
The coldness hits my chest

Exhausted and frustrated
I stumbled to the door
Standing, upset and frightened
Your bear was on the floor

I quickly picked you up
And gave you back your bear
You reached up toward my head
And ran your hands through my hair

You stared into my eyes
A moment, forever, I hoped would last
A mirror stood between us,
Reflecting your future and my past

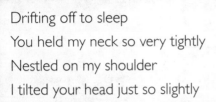

Drifting off to sleep
You held my neck so very tightly
Nestled on my shoulder
I tilted your head just so slightly

Never have I known
A moment so tender and so sweet
A warmth flushed my body
Your comfort spawned the heat

Now I'll lay you down
So you can dream of days ahead
I'll tuck you in so softly
So tenderly in your bed

I'll always be there for you
No matter what, where or when
But now I must get my rest
For soon, you'll have me up again[21]

Today ...

Tomorrow ...

Write down your thoughts and goals.

> *Let the little children come to me, and do not hinder them; for to such belongs the kingdom of heaven.*
> *— Matthew 19:14 (RSV)*

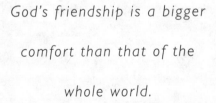

God's friendship is a bigger

comfort than that of the

whole world.

— Martin Luther

THE BUSY FATHER

The sickly English boy was born in 1874, to well-to-do parents. They were remote, however, at least emotionally. Sometimes physically. The boy often didn't see them for long stretches, even during holidays. The father, aloof. The mother, self-absorbed.

It was said that his own childhood "was horribly lacking in affection."

As he grew up, he followed in his own father's footsteps, and actually accomplished more. But he did lack one of his father's attributes: the aloofness.

Success — and momentous times — carried him along the winds of history. His own country needed him in ways no one could have imagined. Yet his own children were never far from his thoughts. Not even in the darkest moments of war.

Winston Churchill, you see, loved his children. His son Randolph, reflecting on a holiday conversation with his father, said that the old lion told him they had just talked more than he had talked with his father . . . ever.

How about it, Dad? Are you too successful, too busy, to spend time with your children? If so, that is a future regret you want no part of. Even if the weight of the world is on your shoulders, make room for your children to ride on those same shoulders, to laugh, and to make memories.

TODAY...

TOMORROW...

Write down your thoughts and goals.

And he arose and came to his father. But when he was still a great way off, his father saw him and had compassion, and ran and fell on his neck and kissed him.

– Luke 15:20

One father is worth more than a

hundred school masters.

– George Herbert

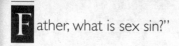

Father, what is sex sin?"

My father turned to look at me, as he always did when answering a question, but to my surprise he said nothing. At last he stood up, lifted his traveling case from the rack over our heads, and set it on the floor.

"Will you carry it off the train, Corrie?" he said. I stood up and tugged at it. It was crammed with the watches and spare parts he had purchased that morning.

"It's too heavy," I said.

"Yes," he said. "And it would be a pretty poor father who would ask his little girl to carry such a load. It's the same way, Corrie, with knowledge.

Some knowledge is too heavy for children. When you are older and stronger you can bear it. For now you must trust me to carry it for you."

And I was satisfied. More than satisfied — — wonderfully at peace. There were answers to this and all my hard questions — but now I was content to leave them in my father's keeping.[22]

TODAY ...

TOMORROW ...

Write down your thoughts and goals.

Bear ye one another's burdens....
– Galatians 6:2

A burden shared is a lighter load.

– Anonymous

THAT AGE-OLD QUESTION

It's a lazy Sunday afternoon, and my five-year-old son, Stephen, and I are sprawled across the couch. I'm reading aloud from C.S. Lewis' *Chronicles of Narnia*, and my boy is lapping up every word. With each page, he studies my every inflection. Ah, quality time.

"Daddy," my blond son interrupts. "You're getting old."

"What did you say, Stephen?"

"You kinda look like Grandpa," he replies.

My son's blue eyes are scrutinizing me, searching for signs of age.

"What do you mean, I look like Grandpa?" I try to remain calm, but inside I'm losing it.

"You have lines on your head."

"No, I don't ... Do I?"

"Yep."

"Where?"

"Here, here and here. You're getting old."

Oh, boy. I didn't need to hear this.

"Do you think I'm going to die soon, Stephen?"

"I don't know. How many are you?"

"I'm 30 years old. Remember? I just blew out 30 candles on my cake — or at least, most of them?

"How many is 30?"

"Well, it's this many three times," I say, showing him my hands with all the fingers outstretched.

His blue eyes are really big now. "Yep, you're old."

Now, I realize it doesn't take a rocket scientist to determine that the crown of my head bears a striking resemblance to a mosquito landing zone. But until now, I thought I was doing all right. After all, 40 years is old, not 30. No way. As I straighten up on the couch, the sad truth begins to sink in:

I am 30. Three-oh, no longer a kid. No longer do the neighborhood children call me "Phil." To them, I'm "Mr. Callaway." The college and up-and-coming pro athletes aren't my contemporaries. They're kids.

What do I have to show for three decades on plant earth? It's not incredible wealth. We have a car that's paid for, but the house is a rental. Like most folks, we're just plugging along. Now that I'm "old," I realize wealth is not measured in things you can touch. Fame never got anyone to heaven.

What is worth leaving is my faith in Jesus Christ. Yes, Stephen, that is what I want to leave you. We are rich, my son. Rich in relationships. Rich in memories. Rich in fun. I may not look that good in the will, but for someone approaching retirement age at light speed, it's worth smiling about.[23]

The just man walketh in his integrity: his children are blessed after him.
– Proverbs 20:7

Today ...

_____

_____

_____

_____

_____

_____

_____

_____

_____

_____

Tomorrow ...

_____

_____

_____

_____

Write down your thoughts and goals.

REFERENCES

[1] Erma Bombeck, *Field Enterprises.*

[2] John A. Stroman, *God's Downward Mobility*, (Lima, Ohio:CSS Publishing Company), 1996.

[3] President Abraham Lincoln's Proclamation for a National Day of Fasting, Humiliation and Prayer, April 30, 1863.

[4] Dr. Roger Ray, Sermon: "Written in Stone."

[5] Dwight D. Eisenhower.

[6] Craig Brian Larson, *750 Engaging Illustrations for Preachers, Teachers, and Writers* (Grand Rapids, MI: Baker Books, 2002), p. 75.

[7] Craig Brian Larson, *750 Engaging Illustrations for Preachers, Teachers, and Writers* (Grand Rapids, MI: Baker Books, 2002), p. 108.

[8] "Have a Good Day" vol. 30, no. 12, April 1998.

[9] Ann Landers.

[10] *Homemade*, February, 1989.